W9-AFH-885

BATTLE of the IRONCLADS

The MONITOR and the MERRIMACK

BATTLE of the IRONCLADS

The MONITOR *and the* MERRIMACK

Alden R. Carter

Franklin Watts New York / Chicago / London / Sydney A First Book

FOR FOUR BROTHER OFFICERS FROM LONG AGO:

Joe Hognander
Dick Beamgard
Bill Wright
Don Westerhaus

Photographs copyright ©: Cover: Bettmann Archive; 3: Monitor National Marine Sanctuary; 7, 11, 14, 17, 19 (middle and bottom), 28, 33, 34, 39, 46, 50, 52-53, 55: North Wind Picture Archives; 12-13, 14, 21, 25, 26, 28, 50; 58, 59: The Newberry Library; 15, 23, 49, 51: MOLLUS-Mass, U.S. Military History Institute, Carlisle Barracks, PA; 19 (top): Brown Brothers; 29: U.S. Military History Institute, Carlisle Barracks, PA; 30: West Point Museum, U.S. Military Academy, New York; 37, 43: No credit; 41: Bettmann Archive; 44-45: The Mariners' Museum

Library of Congress Cataloging-in-Publication Data
Carter, Alden R.
Battle of the ironclads : the Monitor and the Merrimack / by Alden R. Carter.
p. cm. — (A First book)
Includes bibliographical references (p.) and index.
Summary: Examines the construction, battles, and technological and historical impact of the Civil War battleships, the Monitor and the Merrimac.
ISBN 0-531-20091-4 (lib. bdg.)
1. Hampton Roads (Va.), Battle of, 1862—Juvenile literature. 2. Monitor (Ironclad)—Juvenile literature. 3. Merrimack (Frigate)— Juvenile literature. [1. Monitor (Ironclad) 2. Merrimack (Frigate) 3. Hampton Roads (Va.), Battle of, 1862. 4. United States—History—Civil War, 1861-1865—Naval operations.] I. Title. II. Series.
E473.2.C37 1993
973.7'52—dc20 93-417 CIP AC

Printed in the United States of America
6 5 4 3 2 1

CONTENTS

ACKNOWLEDGMENTS

Many thanks to all who helped with *Battle of the Ironclads: The Monitor and the Merrimack*, particularly my editors Lorna Greenberg and E. Russell Primm III; my mother, Hilda Carter Fletcher; and my friends Barbara Feinberg and Dean Markwardt. As always, my wife, Carol, deserves much of the credit.

CHAPTER ONE

THE SHIP THAT WOULDN'T DIE

FLAMES ROARED ACROSS the deck to climb the tall masts of USS *Merrimack*. The great navy yard of Norfolk, Virginia, was burning, the fires set by sailors trying to destroy everything they could not save from the enemy at the gates. Escaping across the harbor, sailors wept as towering flames swallowed ships that they had sailed to the far corners of the earth. More than a few also wept for longtime shipmates who had become enemies as civil war engulfed the nation.

In the spring of 1861, America was at war with itself. Years of bitter argument between North and South over slavery and the rights of individual states had split the nation. The previous fall, Republican presidential candidate Abraham Lincoln (1809–1865) had campaigned against the spread of slavery into the unsettled lands beyond the Mississippi River. His narrow victory set off an uproar in the slave-owning South. South Carolina, Mississippi, Florida, Alabama, Georgia, Louisiana, and Texas quit the Union to form a new nation, the Confederate States of America.

The seceding states grabbed nearly all the army and navy bases within their borders, but Union troops refused to surrender Fort Sumter in the harbor of Charleston, South Carolina. Lincoln took office on March 4, still hoping for a peaceful settlement to the crisis tearing the nation apart. He promised Confederate President Jefferson Davis (1808–1889) that he would send no more troops to Fort Sumter as long as a chance for peace remained.

Lincoln needed time. If he could calm the fears of the eight slave states still in the Union, the seceding states might rejoin in a few weeks or months. Virginia was the richest slave state still to choose between Union and Confederacy. Lincoln ordered his officers in Norfolk to avoid any hostile act that might drive Virginia into the Confederacy.

Norfolk's central location on the Atlantic seaboard made it an ideal home base for the navy of a united nation. From Norfolk the fleet could protect the ports of North and South with equal ease. The naval base itself guarded the entrance of Chesapeake Bay and the dozens of towns and cities, including Baltimore and Washington, D.C., on its shores and along the rivers emptying into the bay.

Norfolk lay on the south shore of Hampton Roads, an 8-mile-long (13-km) channel created by three

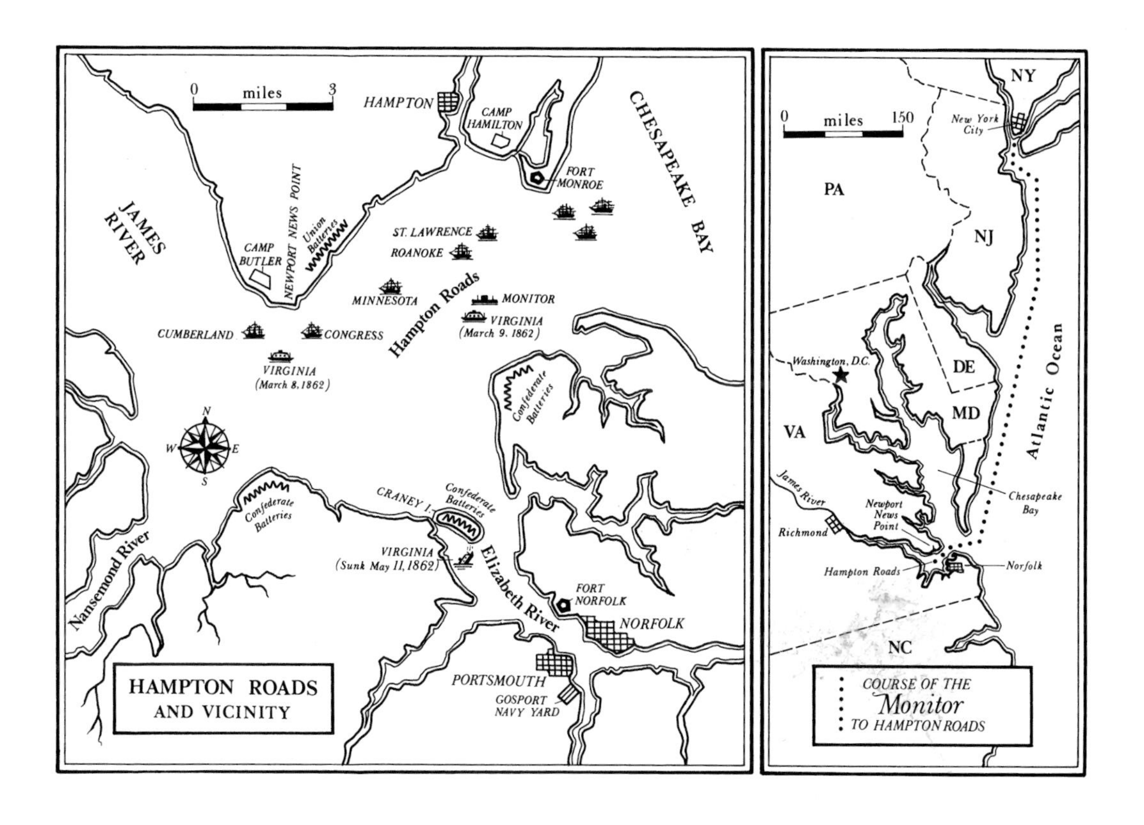

rivers emptying into Chesapeake Bay: the Elizabeth from the south, the Nansemond from the southwest, and the James from the northwest. The Gosport Naval Shipyard stood on the west bank of the Elizabeth, across from the city of Norfolk and just south of the town of Portsmouth. On the north shore of the Roads sat two towns, Newport News to the west and Hampton to the east. Southeast of Hampton, strong Fort Monroe overlooked the outlet of the Roads into Chesapeake Bay.

On the day Lincoln was sworn in as the nation's sixteenth president, ten warships lay along the docks at Gosport. By far the best was the forty-seven-gun frigate *Merrimack*. The five-year-old *Merrimack* had sails to carry it across the open ocean and steam engines for maneuvering in port or in time of faint winds. After thousands of miles of hard duty, its engines needed overhauling. Tied up at Gosport with its guns ashore and its engines torn down, *Merrimack* sat helpless—a mighty prize for the taking.

Lincoln's secretary of the navy, Gideon Welles (1802–1878), ordered *Merrimack* readied for sea, but the orders landed in the unsteady hands of Gosport's commander, Commodore Charles S. McCauley. Although a loyal Union officer, McCauley was an aged, uncertain man, more fond of whiskey than responsibility. His chief engineer worked desperately to get *Merrimack*'s engines repaired. But McCauley, unsure of many of his officers' loyalty and fearful of Norfolk's grumbling population,

THE POWERFUL FRIGATE *MERRIMACK* AT SEA IN THE LATE 1850S. EQUIPPED WITH BOTH SAILS AND STEAM ENGINES, *MERRIMACK* WAS ONE OF THE MOST MODERN WARSHIPS AFLOAT.

found excuse after excuse to delay outfitting the ship with guns and a crew.

On April 12, Confederate cannons in Charleston opened fire on Fort Sumter, destroying any chance for peace. Forced to choose between Union and Confederacy, Virginia voted to secede on April 17. Rumors swept Norfolk of Confederate plans to capture the navy yard. Aboard the newly arrived twenty-four-gun sloop *Cumberland,* Union sailors loaded their cannons and waited for an attack. Exhausted engineers hurried to McCauley with news that *Merrimack*'s engines were at last repaired. They begged McCauley to send the

frigate across the Roads to the safety of Fort Monroe. But McCauley froze, unable to make a decision.

Welles rushed more troops and a new yard commander, Commodore Hiram Paulding, to Norfolk aboard the small sloop *Pawnee*. It docked on the night of April 20, three hours too late; the panicky McCauley had already begun sinking *Merrimack* and the other ships under repair at Gosport. Unable to save the ships or to defend the yard, Paulding ordered his men to destroy everything they could not carry away. The sailors set off with barrels of turpentine and casks of gunpowder to do the dirty, dangerous job.

At 3:30 A.M. on April 21, a tug towed *Cumberland* into the Roads. *Pawnee* followed, as the last sailors

UNION SAILORS SET FIRE TO *MERRIMACK* AND SEVEN OTHER SHIPS AT THE GOSPORT NAVY YARD AS CONFEDERATE TROOPS PREPARED TO STORM THE NAVAL BASE AT NORFOLK, VIRGINIA, ON APRIL 21, 1861.

ashore lit the fires and ran for their boats. Minutes later, flames roared across the yard, and explosions hurled wreckage high into the night sky. For a few minutes, the masts of *Merrimack* stood silhouetted against the fires, then the mighty frigate burst into flame.

One of the great warships of the age died that night, but from the sunken wreck of *Merrimack* a new and terrifying ship would be born—a creeping iron monster that would blast tall ships and then face another ironclad in the most famous single-ship duel in naval history.

CHAPTER TWO

IRONCLAD MONSTERS

CONFEDERATE Secretary of the Navy Stephen Mallory (1813–1873) commanded a navy that hardly existed. Except for a few gunboats, the South had no warships to protect 3,500 miles (5,650 km) of coastline from Hampton Roads, Virginia, to Brownsville, Texas. With the war only weeks old, Union warships already cruised off the Confederacy's ports, and Union Secretary of the Navy Welles was buying and arming civilian ships by the score to strengthen the blockade.

With few factories to make the tools of war, the South needed to trade its cotton in Europe for everything from uniforms to gunpowder. Unless Mallory found a way to break the blockade, the South would die a slow death. Mallory could not match Welles ship for ship, but perhaps he could build an ironclad monster that would turn the wooden ships of the Union navy into so much kindling.

The idea of an iron-plated warship dated back centuries, and the Koreans had actually built an ironclad in 1592. But the world's major navies rejected the idea

CONFEDERATE SECRETARY OF THE NAVY STEPHEN MALLORY FACED THE DIFFICULT TASK OF BREAKING THE UNION BLOCKADE OF THE SOUTH'S PORTS.

until the 1850s, when new long-range guns and improved explosive shells threatened to make stout wooden hulls obsolete. Reluctantly, European navies began experimenting with ironclads. During the Crimean War (1854–56), the French navy used three armored gun batteries to destroy a Russian fort. In 1859, France launched *Gloire*, the world's first seagoing ironclad. A year later, Britain answered with *Warrior*, the first all-iron warship.

On June 3, 1861, Mallory gave the job of building a Confederate ironclad to dashing thirty-five-year-old Lt. John Brooke. Brooke recruited two other former U.S. naval officers, ship-constructor Lt. John Porter and engineer Lt. William Williamson. Because the Confederacy had neither the time nor the shipyards to build an ironclad from the keel up, they decided to raise the sunken hull of the once-proud *Merrimack.*

Confederate work crews at Gosport refloated the frigate and towed its hulk into the yard's huge stone dry dock. Porter cut away the charred upper works and started building a long, slanted shed, called a "casemate," on a new gun deck. Brooke set about designing iron plates to cover the thick planking of the casemate in crisscrossing layers. The casemate would protect ten big guns: one each at bow and stern and four-gun "broadsides" along each side.

The reborn *Merrimack* was renamed *Virginia,* although even some of its own crew continued to use the

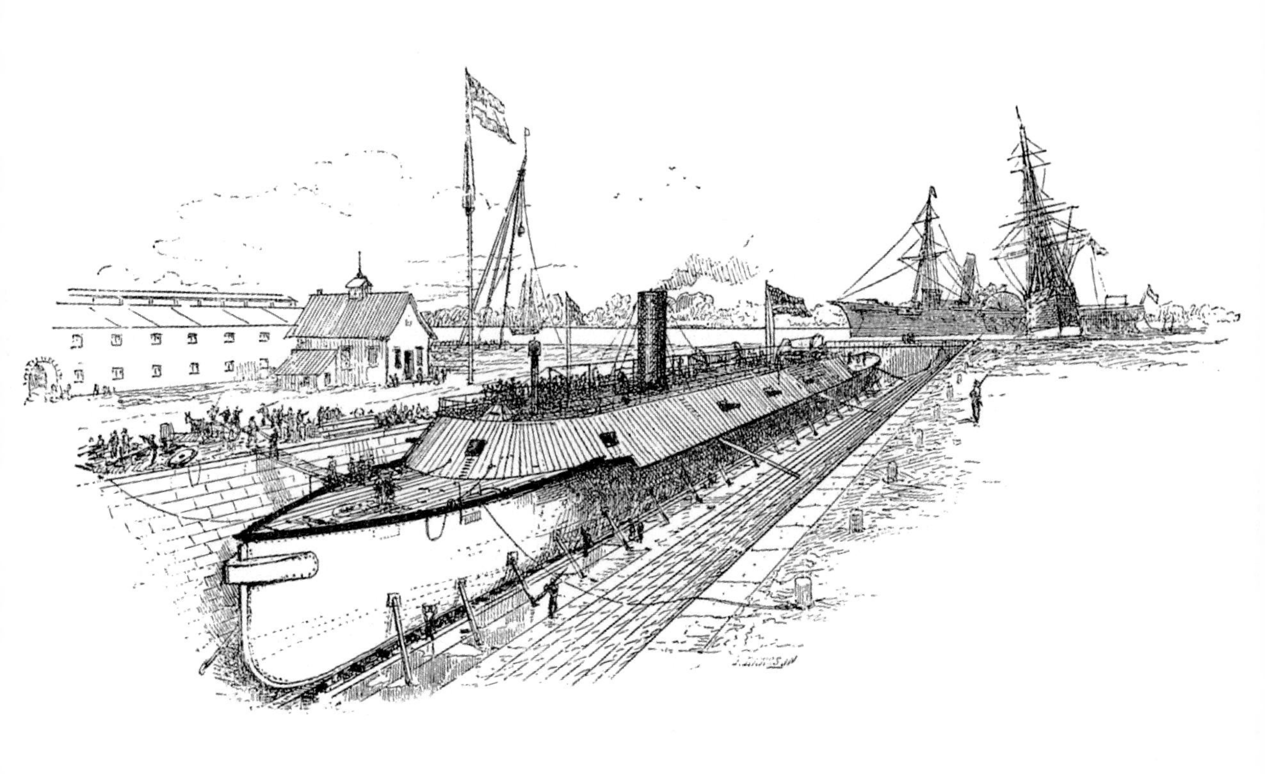

RAISED FROM THE HARBOR MUD, THE HULL OF *MERRIMACK* WAS REBUILT UNDER THE DIRECTION OF LT. JOHN BROOKE AS THE CONFEDERATE IRONCLAD CSS *VIRGINIA*.

old name. The work was well underway when Confederate soldiers defeated a Union army at Manassas Junction, Virginia, on July 21 in the first major battle of the war. Two days later, the Tredegar Iron Works in Richmond, Virginia, began making *Virginia*'s 723 tons (657 metric tons) of iron plates.

Northern spies sent Welles news of the ironclad monster the Confederates were building in Norfolk. Welles hurried to counter the Confederate challenge. He placed a newspaper advertisement calling for ironclad designs and appointed an Ironclad Board of three senior officers to choose the best two or three.

In New York City, a crusty Swedish genius dusted off plans for an ironclad. John Ericsson (1803–1889) was one of the great inventors of the Industrial Revolution sweeping Europe and America. He had designed dozens of machines to harness iron and steam for the service of humankind. In 1843, he had built USS *Princeton*, the most advanced warship of the day. But the navy had unfairly blamed Ericsson when a gun exploded aboard the ship, killing several important men. Still bitter in 1861, Ericsson wrote to Lincoln rather than the Navy Department. The letter got lost and, on receiving no reply, a disgusted Ericsson shelved his plans.

Fortunately for the Union, Cornelius Bushnell, a young shipbuilder, dropped by Ericsson's office to discuss ironclads. Ericsson showed him a model for a ship unlike anything the world had ever seen. Identically tapered at bow and stern, *Monitor* would have a flat-bottomed iron hull bolted to an iron-plated wooden raft floating only 18 inches (46 cm) above the water. In the center of the raft would sit a two-gun rotating turret armored with eight layers of 1-inch (2.5-cm) iron plate.

(TOP) THE PRICKLY SWEDISH ENGINEER JOHN ERICSSON DESIGNED AND BUILT USS *MONITOR* TO ANSWER THE CHALLENGE OF CSS *VIRGINIA*. (MIDDLE AND BOTTOM) ERICSSON'S QUICK PENCIL SKETCH OF HIS IDEA FOR AN IRONCLAD SHIP EVENTUALLY DEVELOPED INTO THE FULL-DETAIL DIAGRAM OF *MONITOR*.

The two men became partners. Bushnell set off immediately to show Secretary Welles and the president Ericsson's design. The politicians were impressed, but the Ironclad Board—recalling the navy's stormy relationship with Ericsson—turned it down. Bushnell rushed back to New York, told Ericsson that the board had a few small questions, and convinced the inventor to go to Washington. Arriving at the Navy Department on September 15, Ericsson was astounded to learn that the board had disapproved his entire plan. He leaped to *Monitor*'s defense, delivering a dazzling lecture that reversed the board's vote.

Ericsson threw himself into the labor of building *Monitor*. The Confederates had a three-month head start on their ironclad, and Ericsson called on the industrial strength of the North to even the race. The Continental Iron Works in Brooklyn, New York, built the hull and added the iron plates, boiler, machinery, guns, and turret as they arrived from factories as far away as New Hampshire. As *Monitor* took shape in Continental's vast ship house, Ericsson was a "high-pressure steam engine" of energy as he drove the work crews to superhuman effort.

Northern newspapers published plans of the ship and described many of the forty new inventions Ericsson had designed for *Monitor*. The Confederates had no better luck keeping their secrets out of print, as Southern

THE IRONCLADS BECAME THE SUBJECT OF WIDE PUBLIC INTEREST IN BOTH NORTH AND SOUTH. *HARPER'S WEEKLY* PUBLISHED THESE DETAILS OF *MONITOR*'S DESIGN IN ITS APRIL 1862 ISSUE.

newspapers published frequent reports on the rush to complete *Virginia.*

On January 30, 1862—only ninety-seven days after the start of construction—*Monitor* slid down the greased beams leading from the ship house into New York harbor. A small crowd of spectators held their breath. Some newspapers had labeled *Monitor* "Ericsson's Folly" and predicted that it would sink like a stone. But, as Ericsson had promised, *Monitor* "floated like a duck."

Monitor's captain led his nine officers and forty-seven sailors on board. At forty-four, Lt. John Worden was a slender, soft-spoken man, his skin still pale from seven months in a Confederate prison camp. He had great confidence in *Monitor* and its volunteer crew. Together, they could stop *Virginia*—if they could get to Hampton Roads in time. Maintaining the blockade of Norfolk had become even more important with the new year of 1862. In the spring, Gen. George McClellan (1826–1885) planned to land a huge Union army on the *Virginia* shore of Chesapeake Bay for an overland attack on the Confederate capital at Richmond. But *Virginia* could ruin the entire plan if it drove the blockading ships from the Roads and steamed north to destroy McClellan's unarmed transport ships.

Worden and his men knew that much depended on them. They worked from dawn until long past dark to master their novel and untried ship. They loaded coal,

LT. JOHN WORDEN VOLUNTEERED TO COMMAND *MONITOR*, A WARSHIP THOUGHT SO UNSEAWORTHY THAT NEWSPAPERS LABELED IT "ERICSSON'S FOLLY."

ammunition, and food, took *Monitor* on test runs, and corrected dozens of problems left behind by the hurried work crews. Secretary Welles sent increasingly anxious messages to Worden, urging him to get *Monitor* ready for sea.

Welles knew that the Confederates were doing everything possible to finish *Virginia* before the Union could send its ironclad to Hampton Roads. Confederate President Davis and Secretary Mallory had great hopes for *Virginia.* The splintering of the blockade and the foiling of McClellan's great invasion could turn the tide of war. Many Northerners would renounce Lincoln and his war policies. France and Britain, the South's major trading partners, might recognize the Confederacy's independence and perhaps even send their navies to protect the South's ports. Under pressure from foreign powers and Northern voters, Lincoln would have to make peace.

But Brooke and his team in Norfolk were having problems. Dissatisfied with the strength of three layers of 1-inch (2.5-cm) iron plate on *Virginia*'s casemate, Brooke had ordered two layers of 2-inch (5-cm) armor. But the Tredegar Iron Works had difficulty making the plates and even more problems shipping them to Norfolk over the Confederacy's creaking railroads. Brooke's frequent changes worsened his touchy relationship with Porter, who had crews working on the ship around the clock. Below decks Williamson labored, unable to promise either speed or reliability from the ship's worn-out engines.

On February 17, 1862, the gates of the dry dock opened. As water flooded in, many onlookers expected to

see *Virginia* sink straight to the bottom. But the big, ugly ship floated. *Virginia* was a third longer than *Monitor* and weighed four times as much. It needed at least 22 feet (6.7 m) of water to maneuver, more than twice the draft of *Monitor*—a great disadvantage in shallow Hampton Roads. Still, no matter how clumsy, slow, and deep-draft, *Virginia* was a fearsome weapon. On March 7, with shipyard workers still hammering on the casemate, Commodore Franklin Buchanan told his crew of thirty officers and three hundred enlisted volunteers that *Virginia* would steam into the Roads on the following day.

VIRGINIA STEAMED INTO HAMPTON ROADS ON MARCH 8, 1862, TO DELIVER A DEVASTATING ATTACK ON THE TALL WOODEN WARSHIPS OF THE UNION BLOCK ADING SQUADRON.

THE COMPLETED *MONITOR* WAS RUSHED TO HAMPTON ROADS, NARROWLY SURVIVING THE STORMY PASSAGE FROM NEW YORK.

As *Virginia*'s crew prepared for sea, *Monitor* was in serious trouble on the stormy Atlantic. *Monitor* had steamed out of New York harbor on the afternoon of March 6. At the end of a long towline from the tug *Seth Low*, *Monitor* made good speed through calm seas. But the weather changed toward evening on March 7. *Monitor* began pitching heavily. Waves rolled across the low deck to crash against the turret. A "waterfall" streamed through the joint between turret and deck. More water washed down the smokestack and into the blower vents bringing air to the boiler room. The blowers shut down, and poisonous gases spread from the fires through the ship. Men collapsed and were hauled barely alive to the top of the turret.

The untended pumps failed, and water rose into the boiler room. Worden formed a bucket line to bail the water, while his second in command, twenty-three-year-old Lt. S. Dana Greene, signaled *Seth Low* to turn shoreward. After five desperate hours, *Monitor* reached smoother waters where the blowers and pumps could be fixed. But late that night, the ship again hit rough seas and again the crew had to work like madmen to save their lives and the ship.

Monitor entered Chesapeake Bay on the afternoon of March 8. In the distance, its exhausted crew saw puffs of smoke over Hampton Roads and heard the thunder of distant gunfire. As night fell, the glow of a burning ship lit the sky. The mighty *Virginia* had struck.

CHAPTER THREE

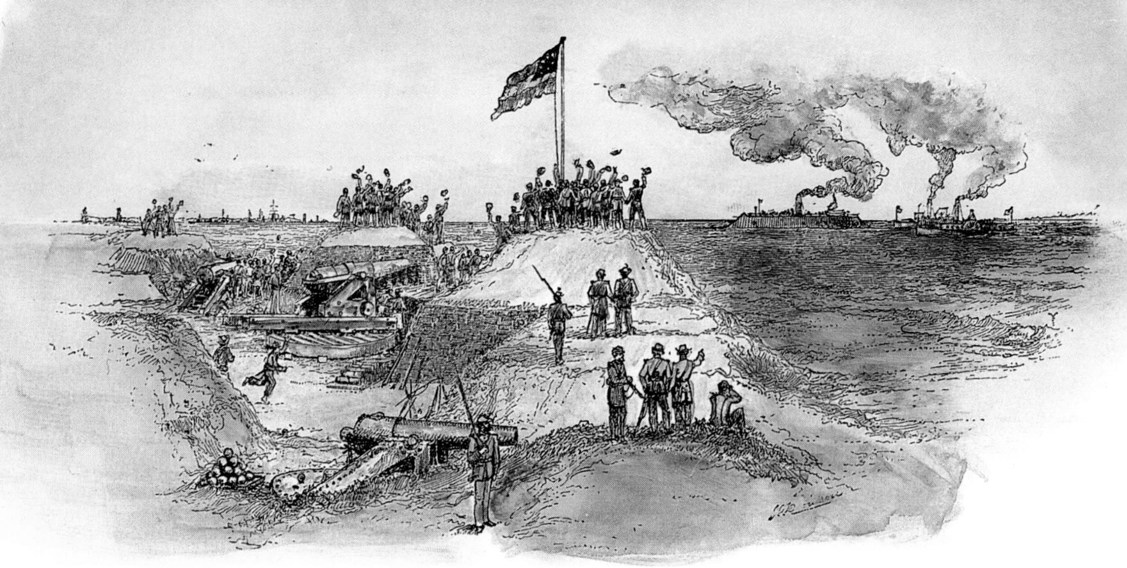

DEATH OF THE TALL SHIPS

SILENT CROWDS watched as *Virginia* steamed down the Elizabeth River into Hampton Roads late in the morning of March 8, 1862. To townspeople long used to the sight of tall, graceful sailing ships, the grunting, spark-spewing ironclad looked like an iron coffin destined to sink with its crew and the hopes of the Confederacy. Then someone gave a faint cheer. Others took it up until the cheering spread through the crowd—a wave of hope and pride in the ship and the sailors going forth to face the South's enemies.

Five large Union warships were anchored on the far side of the Roads. The old fifty-gun sail frigate *St. Lawrence* and the new forty-seven-gun steam frigates *Roanoke* and *Minnesota*—sisters of the original *Merrimack*—lay to the east near Fort Monroe. To the west, the old fifty-gun sail frigate *Congress* and the smaller but more powerful twenty-four-gun sail sloop *Cumberland* guarded the mouth of the James River near Newport News. On *Congress,* a lookout studied a column of smoke rising above the Elizabeth, then turned to an officer: "Sir, I think that thing is a-comin' down at last."

As *Virginia* puffed into the Roads, Commodore Buchanan picked his first target: *Cumberland*, rumored to have heavy new guns. Followed by two lightly armed

COMMODORES FRANKLIN BUCHANAN AND JOSIAH TATTNALL, FIRST AND FINAL COMMANDERS OF *VIRGINIA*.

SIDE RIPPED OPEN BY THE CONFEDERATE RAM, *CUMBERLAND* SINKS UNDER THE POUNDING OF *VIRGINIA*, WHILE IN THE BACKGROUND THE TUG *ZOUAVE* TRIES TO TOW THE WOUNDED *CONGRESS* TO SAFETY.

steamers, *Virginia* swung toward Newport News. Hurrying to investigate the mysterious column of smoke, the captain of the Union tug *Zouave* saw what "looked like the roof of a very big barn belching forth smoke." He fired his small cannon a few times at *Virginia,* then turned back to spread the alarm. The Union warships became a flurry of activity as sailors pulled wash from the rigging, cleared decks, and loaded guns. *Minnesota* got underway with its steam engines, but in the light wind, *Roanoke* (its engines out of order) and *St. Lawrence* had to call for tugs.

Virginia plowed slowly toward *Cumberland,* its forward deck just clearing the water and looking to one Union officer like "a huge half-submerged crocodile." A flash from its forward gun sent a shell smashing into *Cumberland.* The Union gunners fired back, desperately trying to disable the approaching monster. *Congress* fired a broadside as *Virginia* passed, but the cannonballs bounced off the ironclad's slanting casemate like so many marbles. *Virginia*'s answering broadside ripped through *Congress*'s sides and set the old frigate on fire.

Virginia bore down on *Cumberland,* its exploding shells tearing huge holes in the sloop. Screaming iron fragments and hissing wood splinters killed or terribly wounded dozens of Union sailors. With a tremendous crash, *Virginia*'s 1,500-pound (680-kg) ram drove into the side of *Cumberland,* tearing a hole big enough "to drive in a horse and cart." Buchanan put his engines full astern, trying to wrench the ram free as the sinking sloop began dragging *Virginia* down. The two ships swung together, their guns nearly touching, their crews blazing away at each other. With a shriek of metal, the ram broke.

Virginia backed away, pouring shells into the dying ship from a range of 20 feet (6 m). The Union crews stuck to their guns, their feet slipping on the bloody, slanting decks as *Cumberland* heeled over. They fired until the water rose to the guns before finally abandoning ship. *Cumberland* settled into the harbor mud, its mast tops above water, its flags still flying.

Virginia began an upstream turn, as three Confederate gunboats dashed down the James to join the battle. Union guns ashore blazed away at the Confederate ships, while the plucky *Zouave* struggled to tow the crippled *Congress* into shallow water where the deep-draft ironclad could not go. Swinging ponderously about, *Virginia* took thirty minutes to complete the turn, but *Congress* could not get away. From a range of 200 yards (180 m), *Virginia* slammed shell after shell into the stern of *Congress*. The Union sailors fought back until a horrified witness on *Zouave* saw blood running over the frigate's sides "like water on a wash-deck morning." Finally, its stern guns destroyed, *Congress* lowered its flag.

UNABLE TO ESCAPE *VIRGINIA*, THE FRIGATE *CONGRESS* IS SET ABLAZE BY "HOTSHOT."

Buchanan ordered two of the gunboats to go alongside *Congress* to accept the surrender. But on shore, Union Gen. Joseph Mansfield roared, "The . . . ship has surrendered, but we haven't!" The storm of Union bullets drove the gunboats away. Enraged, Buchanan grabbed a rifle and started firing shoreward from the open top deck of *Virginia*. A Union bullet hit him in the thigh.

SAILORS LEAP FOR THEIR LIVES FROM THE DECKS OF THE BURNING *CONGRESS*.

Bleeding heavily, Buchanan was carried below. Lt. Catesby Jones, *Virginia*'s executive officer, took command. Following Buchanan's parting order, Jones called for "hotshot." His gunners fired red-hot cannonballs into *Congress,* kindling a half-dozen fires aboard the old frigate. Union sailors who could save themselves leaped overboard, leaving the wounded screaming in the spreading flames.

Virginia swung to the west in search of another target. The three Union frigates trying to come to the aid of *Cumberland* and *Congress* had run aground in the shallows on the north side of the Roads. Tugs pulled *Roanoke* and *St. Lawrence* free and towed them back toward Fort Monroe, but *Minnesota* was stuck fast. As Jones steered toward the Union squadron's stranded flagship, his civilian pilots warned him that *Virginia,* too, risked running aground as the tide ebbed.

Jones surveyed his exhausted ship. The bow was leaking badly where the ram had torn away in *Cumberland*'s side. Union cannonballs had blown the muzzles off two guns, and shell fragments coming through the gun ports had killed two men and wounded another eight. Everything on the upper deck—lifeboats, flag staffs, and two light field guns—had been shot away. The smokestack and vent pipes were riddled with holes, reducing air to the fires and cutting *Virginia*'s speed from 6 to 4 knots. Reluctantly, Jones decided against risking another attack. After lobbing a couple of long-range shots at *Minnesota, Virginia* turned for the south shore of the Roads.

Virginia anchored off Sewell's Point. Jones inspected the ship, counting ninety-eight dents where cannonballs had struck the casemate. Across the Roads, flames enveloped *Congress.* About midnight, the tall ship exploded, signaling the end of the long centuries when wooden warships ruled the oceans of the world. Watching from the top deck, one of *Virginia*'s pilots caught a brief glimpse of a low, oddly shaped ship gliding toward *Minnesota* through the shadows cast on the waters by the flames. *Monitor* had come to Hampton Roads.

CHAPTER FOUR

BATTLE OF THE IRONCLADS

PRESIDENT LINCOLN called his cabinet together at 6:30 A.M. on Sunday, March 9, 1862. The overnight messages from Hampton Roads were grim: *Cumberland* and *Congress* sunk, nearly 250 Union sailors dead, and *Minnesota* grounded—a sitting duck for *Virginia.* Secretary of War Edwin Stanton (1814–1869) stalked the room, pausing at the window to predict that *Virginia* would soon be hurling shells from the Potomac River into the White House itself.

Secretary Welles calmly disagreed, stating that the deep-draft *Virginia* could not make it through the shallows downriver from Washington. Besides, he had word that *Monitor* had arrived safely in Hampton Roads. Stanton demanded to know how many guns *Monitor* carried. Told that it had two, he exploded. Two guns against the mighty *Virginia*? *Virginia* would shoot *Monitor* to pieces, sink every remaining ship in the Union squadron, and then steam north to destroy Washington and every city on the coast. The president must declare an emergency, close every seaport, and block the Potomac with sunken barges.

Lincoln hesitated. He supposed that there would be no harm in strengthening the coastal forts, but he didn't want to close the Potomac just when transports were gathering in the river to carry Gen. McClellan's army south for the landing on the Virginia coast. Stanton could get the barges ready, but he was not to sink them until there was more news from Hampton Roads.

While the president's men argued, Lt. Jones was steering *Virginia* through lifting fog toward the tall silhouette of the stranded *Minnesota*. Along both shores of the Roads, soldiers and civilians gathered to watch what nearly all thought would be the end of the Union flagship. Then *Virginia*'s lookouts spotted a strange vessel—"a cheesebox on a raft"—sliding from *Minnesota*'s shadow. One guessed that it was a barge carrying *Minnesota*'s

THE TINY *MONITOR* STEAMS INTO HAMPTON ROADS TO RESCUE THE WOODEN SHIPS OF THE UNION SQUADRON FROM THE FURY OF THE IRONCLAD *VIRGINIA*.

boiler to shore for repairs. Another thought that it was a floating water tank. Jones suspected the truth: he was about to face Ericsson's *Monitor*.

Monitor had come alongside *Minnesota* shortly after midnight in the light of the burning Congress. Worden found *Minnesota* badly injured from a shell hit by *Virginia* and many more by the Confederate gunboats. Desperate attempts had failed to lighten the flagship enough for a tug to pull it free, and the crew was preparing to fight to the last gun before blowing up *Minnesota*.

Worden readied his ship for battle. No one on board had slept more than snatches in the two days *Monitor* had fought for life on the stormy Atlantic. Yet everyone fell to willingly. Lt. Greene, who would direct the gun crews, asked permission to use full powder charges to propel *Monitor*'s solid shot, rather than the half loads authorized by the navy. Worden refused to risk an explosion that would cripple his guns and ship.

As the eastern sky lightened and the fog lifted, word came that *Virginia* was in sight. Worden took his station in the low pilothouse near the bow, as Greene hurried to the turret. *Monitor* slid out from behind *Minnesota* and steamed straight for *Virginia*.

Paying no attention to the little Union ironclad, *Virginia* opened a deadly fire on *Minnesota*. Worden held course as the two big ships sent broadsides thundering over *Monitor*. At about 600 yards (550 m), *Monitor*'s turret revolved and its big guns spoke. Two 184-pound (84-kg) cannonballs smashed into *Virginia*'s casemate. One of *Monitor*'s sailors recalled: "You can see surprise on a ship just the same as . . . in a human being, and there was surprise all over the *Merrimack*."

The twin hammer blows of *Monitor*'s 11-inch (28-cm) solid shot forced Jones to turn *Virginia*'s fire away

MONITOR AND *VIRGINIA* SLUG IT OUT IN HISTORY'S FIRST BATTLE OF IRONCLAD WARSHIPS.

from *Minnesota.* The ironclads closed to within 50 yards (45 m). For the next two hours, they blasted away, neither able to do the other much harm. *Monitor* fired every eight minutes, its half-charge cannonballs cracking *Virginia*'s iron plates and pushing in the casemate beams behind, but never breaking through. *Virginia* fired a broadside every five minutes, its powder-filled shells—deadly to wooden ships—exploding harmlessly against *Monitor*'s turret.

Strong as they were, both ships were having problems. *Virginia* had taken a ferocious pounding in its fight with *Cumberland* and *Congress.* Its smokestack and vent pipes riddled, *Virginia* could make barely 4 knots and handled as sluggishly "as Noah's Arc." Water leaking in through the damaged bow increased *Virginia*'s already deep draft, and Jones worried constantly about running aground. The crew worked half naked in nearly unbearable heat, their bodies blackened by coal and powder smoke and their ears deafened by the roar of their own guns and the clang of *Monitor*'s shot striking the casemate walls.

Twice as fast and drawing only half as much water, *Monitor* steamed around the clumsy *Virginia* without danger of running aground. But battle was revealing serious flaws in *Monitor*'s complicated systems. Temperatures in the turret soared to 140° F (60° C) as smoke and heat overtaxed the ventilation equipment.

The voice tube between the pilothouse and turret broke, forcing Worden and Greene to use messengers. The small steam engine that turned the turret proved difficult to operate, and the shutters covering the gun ports between shots were so heavy that it took the entire turret crew to raise and lower them. Forced to leave the shutters up, Greene turned the turret away from *Virginia* to

TEMPERATURES SOARED TO 140° F (100° C) INSIDE *MONITOR*'S TURRET DURING THE BATTLE AGAINST *VIRGINIA*.

reload, and then "fired on the fly" as the turret swung around. Unable to aim properly, he could not hit the same spot on *Virginia*'s casemate twice in a row, where even a half-load shot might well have broken through.

About 10:30 A.M., a frustrated Jones gave the order to steer for *Minnesota.* But the rattled pilot ran the ship aground. *Monitor* swung in to fire at *Virginia*'s stern. *Virginia* lay helpless, unable to return fire because of the angle. Desperate engineers tied down the boilers' safety valves and crammed the fireboxes full. The boiler pres-

A KNIFE-SHAPED *VIRGINIA* IS SHOWN UNDER BOMBARDMENT IN A MAGAZINE ENGRAVING TITLED "THE SPLENDID VICTORY OF THE ERICSSON BATTERY *MONITOR*." IN REALITY, *VIRGINIA* LOOMED OVER *MONITOR* AND NEITHER SIDE COULD CLAIM A CLEAR VICTORY AT THE END OF THE BATTLE.

sure soared over the danger point as the engines strained. The ship lurched and broke free.

As *Virginia* turned again on *Monitor*, Jones raced below to check for damage. He found one gun crew standing idle. "Why are you not firing?" he demanded. The gun captain replied, "Our powder is precious, sir, and . . . I can do *Monitor* as much damage by snapping

EVEN FIRING AT POINTBLANK RANGE,
NEITHER *MONITOR* NOR *VIRGINIA* COULD
LAND A CRIPPLING BLOW.

my fingers at her every five minutes." "Never mind," Jones said, "we are getting ready to ram."

It took Jones an hour to get his sluggish ship aimed straight for *Monitor*. Worden guessed the Confederate plan: "They're going to run us down. [Tell Mr. Greene] to give them both guns." At the last possible moment, Worden skidded *Monitor* out of the way. *Virginia*'s bow glanced off *Monitor*'s stern just as Greene fired both guns. The huge cannonballs slammed into *Virginia*'s casemate, the shock hurling the Confederate gunners to the deck. They stumbled to their feet, bleeding from nose and ears.

The collision had opened wide the leak in *Virginia*'s bow, but Jones refused to give up the fight. When *Monitor* turned into shallow water to resupply the turret's ammunition, Jones again steered toward *Minnesota*. *Virginia*'s shells nearly tore apart the tug *Dragon* alongside *Minnesota* and sent clouds of smoke and splinters erupting from the tall frigate. Then *Monitor* was pushing in between like a collie protecting its sheep.

Again the ironclads closed, their sides bumping as the gunners tried to land the single deadly punch that would end the battle. Jones ordered his men to prepare to board *Monitor*. Worden saw the danger coming: a sea jacket thrown over *Monitor*'s low pilothouse would blind him, and a few wedges hammered under the turret could

bring it to a jolting stop. Just as *Virginia*'s boarding party was about rush from the casemate, Worden swung *Monitor* away.

It was almost noon, the battle nearly four hours old. Worden decided to ram the stern of *Virginia*, hoping to tear away its rudder and propeller. *Monitor* drove in, but lost steering control for a moment. Its bow missed by 2 feet (.6 m), and *Virginia* fired a full broadside at point-blank range. One shell hit the pilothouse where Worden had his eyes to the narrow viewing slit. He reeled back, his face a mass of blood and powder burns. "My eyes," he cried, "I am blind."

While a messenger rushed to the turret for Greene, the enlisted man on the wheel turned *Monitor* into shallow water. Watching *Monitor* go, Jones thought that *Virginia* had won the battle at last. He wanted to make for *Minnesota* yet again, but his officers advised against it. *Virginia* was low on coal and ammunition, its crew exhausted, and its stern riding deep as water flowed aft from the leaking bow. The tide was running out, and the ship risked grounding any minute. Even more dangerous, the settling stern was forcing the bow up, uncovering *Virginia*'s wooden hull where a single hit could sink the ship. Jones hesitated, then reluctantly set course for Gosport.

Aboard *Monitor*, Greene knelt by his wounded captain. Worden calmly gave him command, and then

IN THE AFTERMATH OF BATTLE, *MONITOR*'S CREW RELAXES ON DECK.

let himself be helped to his stateroom. Greene turned *Monitor* back toward *Virginia* only to find the Confederate ironclad steaming away. He wanted to pursue, but Worden had told him to stick close to *Minnesota.* Greene stopped engines and sent *Monitor*'s crew on deck into the warm afternoon sunlight, as a gentle breeze carried away the smoke of history's first battle between ironclad warships.

CHAPTER FIVE

BLOOD, STEAM, AND IRON

CROWDS CHEERED as *Virginia* steamed up the Elizabeth River to Gosport on the afternoon of March 9. But *Virginia* was a badly injured ship. In two days, it had taken at least 150 hits from Union cannonballs, the twenty heaviest from *Monitor*. Confederate work crews guided *Virginia* into dry dock to repair its leaking bow, cracked plates, and overtaxed engines.

Except for the damage to the pilothouse, *Monitor* had shrugged off twenty-two hits from *Virginia*.

OFFICERS INSPECT THE DENTS ON *MONITOR*'S TURRET. THE UNION IRONCLAD SHRUGGED OFF TWENTY-TWO SHELL HITS FROM *VIRGINIA*'S GUNS AND STOOD READY TO RESUME THE BATTLE.

Ericsson's little ship lay in the shadow of Fort Monroe, ready to resume the battle. *Minnesota* was refloated and the blockade of Hampton Roads made tighter with the arrival of several more Union warships.

No one had died in the battle between the ironclads, and only Worden had been seriously injured. He recovered in a friend's home in Washington. Lincoln visited him to hear a firsthand account of the battle. Worden warned the president that *Monitor* could be overwhelmed by boarders. Following Worden's advice, Lincoln ordered Welles not to risk *Monitor* unless a fight was absolutely necessary.

THOUSANDS OF SPECTATORS WATCHED FROM ANCHORED SHIPS AND THE SHORES OF HAMPTON ROADS AS *MONITOR* AND *VIRGINIA* FOUGHT ON THE MORNING OF MARCH 9, 1862. THE THUNDEROUS FOUR-HOUR BATTLE SERVED NOTICE TO THE WORLD THAT THE AGE OF WOODEN WARSHIPS HAD PASSED.

The repaired *Virginia* led a fleet of gunboats laden with boarding parties into Hampton Roads on April 11. But *Monitor* refused to leave the waters near Fort Monroe, where a pack of Union warships waited with guns and rams for the Confederate ironclad. *Virginia* lobbed a single insulting shot *Monitor*'s way and turned for home.

By mid-April, Gen. McClellan's great army had landed north of Fort Monroe and was pushing slowly up

the Yorktown Peninsula toward Richmond. The outnumbered Confederate army pulled out of Norfolk to defend the Confederate capital. The mighty *Virginia* was trapped. Even if the slow, clumsy ironclad could fight its way through the ring of Union ships at the mouth of the Roads, it would have nowhere to go. There never had been the least danger that *Virginia* could attack Washington; it was simply too unseaworthy to survive outside the smooth waters of Hampton Roads. The crew tried to lighten the ship for an escape up the York River to Richmond, but it was no use. In the early morning hours of May 11, they set their ship on fire. About 5 A.M., *Virginia* exploded with a roar that shook the Roads.

Monitor steamed up the York to support McClellan's advance on Richmond. But the cautious McClellan was outwitted by Gen. Robert E. Lee (1807–1870), who drove the Union army from the gates of the city with daring counterattacks. *Monitor* and a new ironclad, *Galena*, covered McClellan's retreat to the York. That fall, *Monitor* was ordered south to join the blockade of Wilmington, North Carolina. Under tow off Cape Hatteras on December 30, 1862, stormy seas swamped *Monitor*, sending it to the bottom with sixteen of its crew.

The Civil War dragged on month after bloody month. The South built twenty-two ironclads modeled on *Virginia*, while the North completed more than sixty ironclads, most of them larger versions of *Monitor*. Equipped with huge 15-inch (380 mm) guns and firing full powder loads, the monitors proved more than a match for *Virginia*'s cousins. The Union navy tightened the blockade, captured most of the South's major ports, and won control of the inland rivers.

John Ericsson designed more than twenty monitors for the Union. His *Montauk* served under the command of a one-eyed skipper, Commander—later Rear Admiral—John Worden. Worden's opponent at Hampton Roads, Lt. Catesby Jones, helped build Confederate ironclads. One of them, *Tennessee*, fought a ferocious battle against a large Union squadron at Mobile

NORTH AND SOUTH RACED TOP BUILD FLEETS OF IRONCLADS. HERE, FOUR OF *MONITOR*'S DESCENDANTS — *MONADNOCK, CANONICUS, MAHOPAC,* AND *SAGUS* — RIDE OUT A GALE OFF THE NORTH CAROLINA COAST IN 1864.

Bay in August 1864 under the command of fiery Admiral Franklin Buchanan.

In April 1865, the battered Confederacy finally surrendered, bringing America's most tragic war to an end. Ten years later, a salvage company raised the remains of *Virginia*. The ship's bell, anchor, and drive shaft were saved from the scrap yard and can be seen in museums today. *Monitor*'s grave lay undiscovered until 1973, when researchers from Duke University located the ship lying upside down in 220 feet (67 m) of water. Too fragile to bring to the surface, the wreck of *Monitor* was designated a marine sanctuary by the United States government.

Some of the monitors built during the Civil War remained in service well into the twentieth century, the last lowering its flag in 1926. By then the world's navies had long since abandoned broadsides, wooden hulls, and billowing sails in favor of turret guns, steel hulls, and powerful steam engines.

The lessons of the duel between *Monitor* and *Virginia* had not been lost on the world. Within days of the battle, the *London Times* wailed that of the Royal Navy's 149 first-class warships, only iron-hulled *Warrior* and *Black Prince* would stand a chance against "little *Monitor*." For the next half century, the great powers devoted immense wealth and energy to building new iron and steel fleets. The low-slung, turreted warships of the new century would trace their design to *Monitor*. They, too, would fade into history as submarines, aircraft carriers, and missile cruisers became the major weapons of modern navies, but the fight between the *Monitor* and the *Virginia/Merrimack* would remain a legendary event in the making of the modern world.

The first battle between ironclads marked the triumph of the Industrial Revolution. The proud wooden navies—and all the centuries of tradition, craftsmanship, and romance they represented—had been swept away by a pair of chugging, smoke-spewing iron monsters. For better or worse, the world turned from the past to measure its future in terms of progress, science, and iron-hard practicality.

THE SHIPS AT A GLANCE

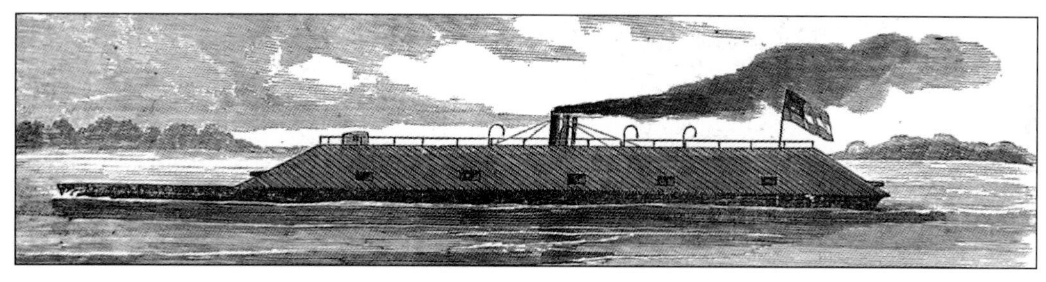

MERRIMACK/VIRGINIA

Length: 273 ft. (83.2 m) + 2.5-ft. (.76-m) iron ram

Width (beam): 38.5 ft. (11.7 m)

Displacement: 4,200 tons (3,800 metric tons)

Draft: 22 ft. (6.7 m)

Gun platform: 172-ft. (52.4-m) x 30-ft. (9.1-m) x 7-ft. (2.1-m) casemate angled at 38 degrees

Armor: two layers of 2-in. (5-cm) iron plate on casemate; single layer of 1-in. (2.5-cm) iron plate on decks; single layer of 1-in. (2.5-cm) iron plate below waterline (incomplete)

Guns: 7-in. (179-mm) Brooke rifles on pivots at bow and stern; three 9-in. (229-mm) smoothbore Dalgrens & one 6-in. (152 mm) Brooke rifle on each broadside

Speed: 6 knots

Crew: 30 officers/300 sailors

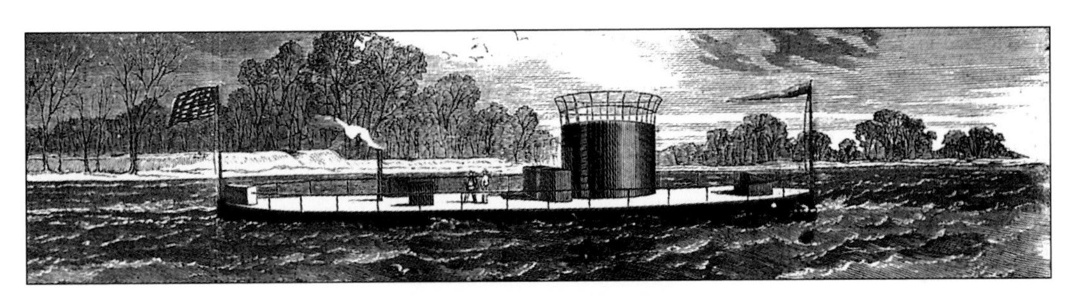

MONITOR

Length: upper hull (the "raft") 172 ft. (52.4 m); lower hull 124 ft. (37.8 m)

Width (beam): upper hull 41.5 ft. (12.6 m); lower hull 34 ft. (10.4 m)

Displacement: 987 tons (896 metric tons)

Draft: 10.5 ft. (3.2 m)

Gun platform: 20-ft. (6.1-m) x 9-ft. (2.7-m) revolving turret

Armor: eight layers of 1-in. (2.5-cm) iron plate on turret; single layer of 1-in. (2.5-cm) iron plate on deck; five layers of 1-in (2.5-cm) iron plate around upper hull

Guns: two 11-in. (279-mm) Dalgren smoothbores

Speed: 7-8 knots

Crew: 10 officers/47 enlisted

FOR FURTHER READING

Carter, Alden R. *The Civil War.* New York: Franklin Watts, 1992.

Catton, Bruce. *The American Heritage Picture History of the Civil War.* New York: Doubleday, 1960.

Davis, William C. *Duel Between the First Ironclads.* New York: Doubleday, 1975.

Donovan, Frank R. *Ironclads of the Civil War.* New York: American Heritage, 1964.

Editors of Time-Life. *The Blockade: Runners and Raiders.* Alexandria, Va.: Time-Life Books, 1987.

Freedman, Russell. *Lincoln: A Photobiography. New York:* Clarion, 1987.

Hoehling, A. A. *Thunder at Hampton Roads.* Englewood Cliffs, N.J.: Prentice-Hall, 1976.

Jordan, Robert Paul. *The Civil War.* Washington, D.C.: National Geographic, 1969.

INDEX

ABOUT THE AUTHOR

ALDEN R. CARTER is a former naval officer and teacher. Since 1984 he has been a writer for children and young adults. His nonfiction books cover a wide range of topics, including titles on electronics, supercomputers, radio, Illinois, Shoshoni Indians, the People's Republic of China, the Alamo, the Battle of Gettysburg, the Colonial Wars, the War of 1812, the Mexican War, the Civil War, the Spanish-American War, and five books on the American Revolution: *The American Revolution: War for Independence; The American Revolution: Colonies in Revolt; Darkest Hours; At the Forge of Liberty;* and *Birth of the Republic.* His novels *Growing Season* (1984), *Wart, Son of Toad* (1985), *Sheila's Dying* (1987), and *Up Country* (1989) were named to the American Library Association's annual list, Best Books for Young Adults. His fifth novel, *RoboDad* (1990), was honored as Best Children's Fiction Book of the Year by the Society of Midland Authors. Mr. Carter lives with his wife, Carol, and their children, Brian Patrick and Siri Morgan, in Marshfield, Wisconsin.